Size Poems

Compiled by John Foster

Contents

Acknowledgements

HarperCollins Publishers, Ltd. for 'Imagine' by Roland Egan from *Have you heard the sun singing?* (Bell and Hyman); Daphne Lister for 'Large and small' from BBC Poetry Corner © 1984 Daphne Lister; John Foster for 'Elephant and ant', 'The giant and the boy', 'Thin and fat' and 'What is long?' all © 1994 John Foster; Irene Yates for 'Giants' © 1994 Irene Yates.

Although every effort has been made to secure copyright permission prior to publication, in a few instances this has not been possible. If notified, the Editor and Publisher will be pleased to rectify any errors or omissions at the earliest opportunity.

Imagine

Imagine a snail
As big as a whale,
Imagine a lark
As big as a shark,

Imagine a cat
As small as a gnat,
And a bee as big as a tree.

Imagine a toad
As long as a road,
Imagine a hare
As big as a chair,

Imagine a goat
As long as a boat,
And a flea the same size as me.

Roland Egan

Large and small

Think of a giant,
Then think of a mouse,
Think of a palace,
Then think of a house,

Think of an eagle,
Then think of a wren,
Think of a wrist watch,
Then think of Big Ben!

Daphne Lister

Elephant and ant

An elephant is so large that it can stand outside my window and blow on my hand.

An ant is so small
that it can crawl
through a tiny crack
in the garden wall.

John Foster

Jack Hall

Jack Hall,
He is so small,
A mouse could eat him,
Hat and all.

Anon

Giants

A giant is only a giant
To someone very small.
And that's why I'll never be
Afraid of a giant at all!

Irene Yates

The giant and the boy

'I'm tall,' said the giant,
'As tall as a tree.
You're short, little boy,
You can't touch my knee.'

'I'm fat,' said the giant.
He gave a big grin.
'I won't gobble you up.
You're much too thin.'

John Foster

Thin and fat

Thin things:
A piece of cotton,
A bit of string,
A drinking straw,
A pencil,
A pin.

Fat things:
A huge tree trunk,
A hippo's belly,
An air balloon,
A giant jelly.

John Foster

What is long?

A river flowing to the sea.
A blue whale.

A runway for a jumbo jet.
A dinosaur's tail.

John Foster

Printed in Hong Kong